ng
Rubbings

Michael Skinner

Studio Vista

Cassell Australia

A Studio Vista/Cassell Australia book

Published in Great Britain by
Studio Vista a division of
Cassell and Collier Macmillan Publishers Limited
35 Red Lion Square, London WC1R 4SG

Sydney, Auckland, Toronto, Johannesburg
an affiliate of the Macmillan Publishing Co. Inc.
New York

Adapted from: How to Make rubbings

First published in this edition 1976

Printed in Great Britain
by Purnell & Sons Ltd., Paulton (Avon) and London

ISBN (Great Britain) 0 289 70708 0

Contents

How to make a simple rubbing

A rubbing is an easy way to make a copy of a surface of an object.

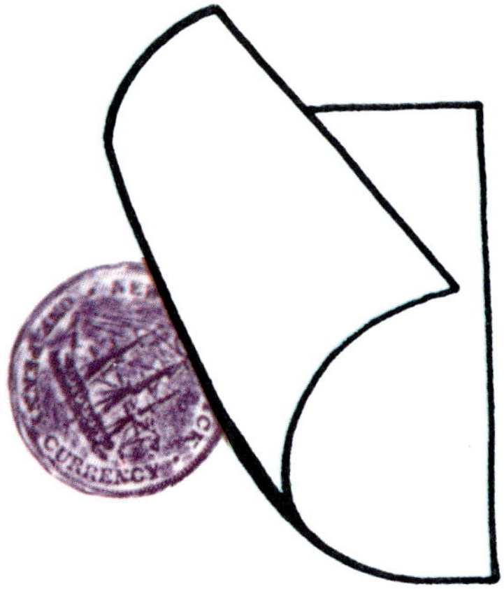

Place an object – a coin, perhaps – under a piece of paper. Then, with a pencil or crayon, 'rub' the surface of the coin through the paper. You will see your copy appearing immediately.

Many ancient, foreign and modern coins, medals and badges have interesting designs.

You could make a collection of kings and queens, for example, or of animals.

Before you start rubbing, fix the underside of each object to the table with adhesive tape.

Cut out your best rubbings and stick them in a note-book, arranging them like a stamp collection.

VICTORIA REGINA

Try rubbing other things using black wax crayon and white paper, not too thick. Hold the paper firmly while you are rubbing so as not to spoil the pattern.

There are many things in the house and garden that make good rubbings. Here are just a few ideas: wood, sandpaper, raised wall-paper, lace, cut glass, book bindings, fossils, string, chain.

Experimenting with different materials

Rubbing on aluminum foil

Ordinary kitchen foil will probably be too thin for some rubbings. Thicker foil may be bought from shops selling artists' materials, and milkbottle tops and disposable metal dishes are ideal for small rubbings.

Lay the foil on the object you wish to rub and fix it in position with masking tape. Work over the area with a nailbrush to press the foil into the pattern underneath. *Never* use foil when rubbing a brass.

If you make a rubbing of a surface or out of doors, wrap the foil around a cardboard tube to avoid creasing it on the way home.

Strengthening and mounting a foil rubbing

Lay the foil face down on a flat surface and cover it with several coats of fibreglass resin or sodium silicate (waterglass). Allow each coat to harden before applying the next.

When it is completely dry, turn the foil over and fill in the lines or grooves by lightly rubbing in liquid shoe polish or lino printing ink, Indian ink, or similar.

When it is dry, clean off any surplus ink by working over the flat areas with fine steel wool.

Your rubbing can now be left as it is or cut out carefully and stuck with quick-drying glue onto dark-coloured cardboard or hardboard. It will also look very effective glued to a door. Be careful not to leave any lumps of glue on the back of the rubbing.

Anno Domin

Making patterns and designs

Leaves

You can make interesting patterns and decorative pictures from leaves. There are hundreds of shapes and sizes from which to choose.

Arrange them first on a piece of paper or card, then stick them down with a quick-drying glue. Lay a sheet of paper on top and then rub, lightly at first, keeping the crayon working in the same direction all the time.

You may like to cut some leaves in half to help the design, or perhaps cut a hole in a leaf to represent an animal's eye.

Odds and ends

See how many different fairly flat objects you can find, such as keys, paper clips, parts of an old clock or toy, safety pins, curtain rings and hooks, chain, washers, matches, string, staples and combs.

Now try arranging them into patterns or decorative animals. Cut a piece of cardboard the size of the design you like best. Cover the card with glue and lay the objects on it one by one. Leave to dry. Now lay a sheet of paper over the design and fix it to the cardboard with adhesive tape before you begin rubbing.

You may prefer to glue only one part of the card at a time, especially if the design is large. Try spreading the glue with a scrap of old thick card. You will find this better than a brush which is difficult to clean if the glue hardens on it.

You can mix several different objects together in your design or use just one kind on their own. If you use string, you may find it necessary to pin it to the cardboard with drawing pins until the glue is dry.

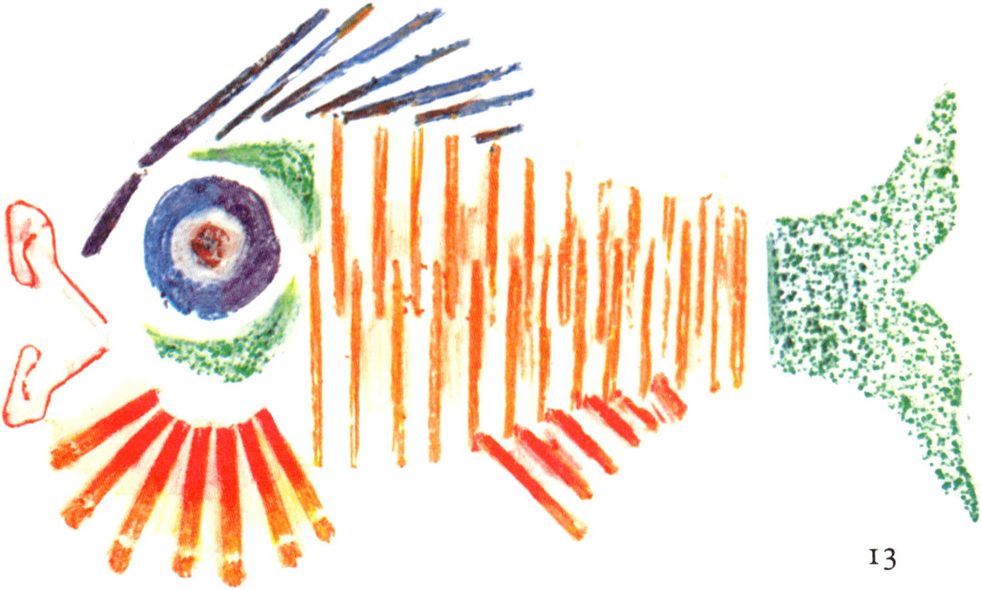

Your name or initials

You need: wax crayon, pencil, paper, cardboard,
scissors, cutting knife and glue

Draw the letters of your name or initials onto the piece of cardboard. If you prefer, you can use the letters printed on an empty food or detergent packet. Whichever you choose, make sure that the card is thicker than the paper you intend to use.

Cut out the letters and try arranging them in different ways, putting some on top of each other. Glue the design you like best onto a piece of cardboard.

Lay a sheet of paper over the top, hold it down firmly, and rub it with crayon.

You can rub the same design over and over again. If it is small enough, you could use it to mark your books or make your own headed notepaper.

Rubbing on fabric

A wide variety of materials are suitable for the making of rubbings – cotton, linen (old sheets or pillow cases), muslin, silk, broadcloth, and many others.

Naturally, the thicker the material you use, the more likely you are to lose some of the detail. It is essential to hold the material firmly in position over the object to be rubbed. Fabric is inclined to stretch, and may distort the design.

The more open or coarse materials give an interesting textured background to the rubbed design, but in this case also it will lose a certain amount of detail.

To 'fix' the crayon, lightly iron the reverse side of the material.

Your designs could be used as patterns for embroidery, or you could use the material for dressing puppets. The possibilities are endless.

Rubbings from fruit and vegetables

Certain fruits and vegetables can make good rubbings. The surface textures themselves can give varied effects. Compare rubbings of a pineapple, an orange and a grapefruit.

It is also possible to make rubbings of the textures inside some fruits and vegetables. First cut them in half or into slices and leave them to dry. Cut them and leave them overnight or place them near direct heat which will help to seal the juices. Make sure you cut straight through the object so as to produce a flat surface for rubbings.

You can make rubbings from apples, pears, carrots, parsnips, cabbages, celery, and many more. Naturally the very soft fruits are not suitable.

Tissue paper and soft wax crayons are usually best for this type of rubbing.

cucumber

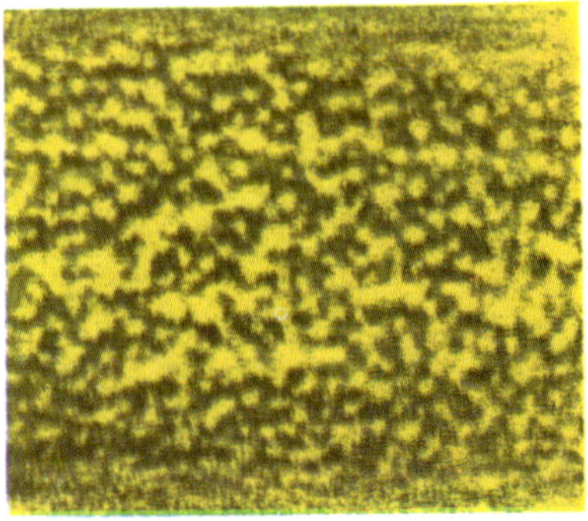

grapefruit

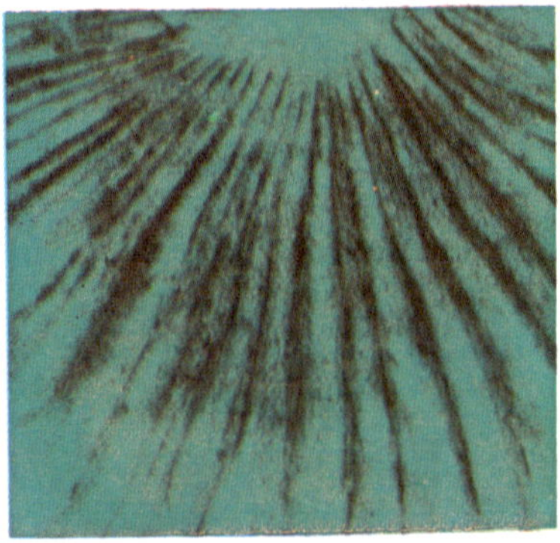

onion

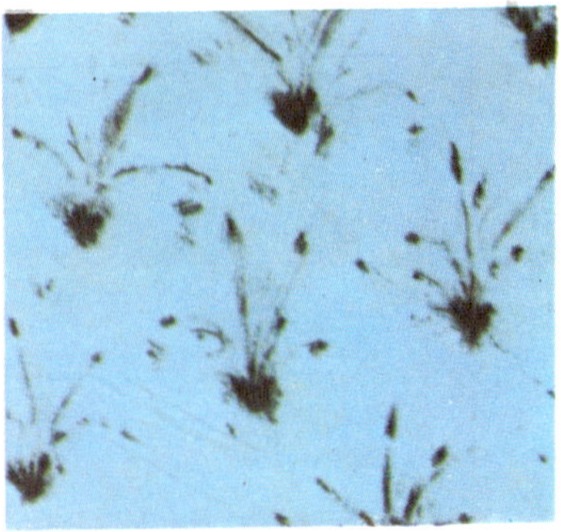

pineapple

parsnip

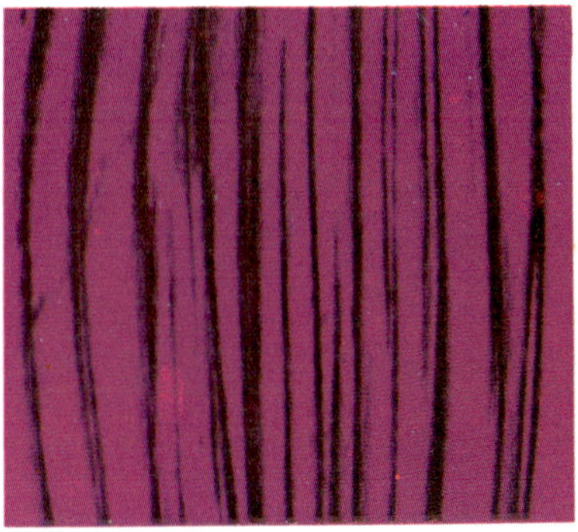

celery

Rubbings from manhole covers

See how many manhole covers you can spot as you walk along the street. Some of them will be very old. And once you have started looking you will be surprised how many different shapes and designs you can find, some of them very beautiful.

Make sure you clean any loose grit or dirt away from the surface with a brush before you start rubbing. Fix the paper with masking tape or hold it down with stones or weights.

Rubbings as interior decoration

Cupboards. This cupboard door is decorated with sections of manhole covers arranged in a circle. Remember that these can be brightly coloured. Cut each section carefully and arrange the pieces on a flat surface, making sure that they fit exactly. Mark the centre of the door. Glue on one section at a time, making sure the point of each section touches the point in the centre of the door. If the cupboard is used a great deal you can cover the rubbings with transparent self-adhesive plastic.

Chest of drawers. The designs you choose could be in one or more colours, and could be the same or different on each drawer. Or, you could rub the names of the items kept in each drawer – games, toys, clothes, for example – using the method described on page 14.

Table mats. Glue some of your designs onto pieces of wood or hardboard. Cover them with transparent self-adhesive plastic.

Headboards. A coat of arms looks very impressive in red, gold or black. Cover the rubbing with self-adhesive plastic, cut it out carefully, and glue or paste it to the headboard.

Waste paper baskets. You can redecorate a basket you already have or find a tin or cardboard container that would be suitable. Simply choose some rubbings to fit your colour scheme, glue them on, and cover the bin with self-adhesive plastic.

Doors. A brass rubbing looks very attractive on a door. Cut the design out carefully and paste it straight onto the door. The paintwork will make a perfect mount or frame.

Many other kinds of rubbings would look good on doors too. Just cut them out and try them. You could also make special designs for each room or rub their names.

Making bookmarks

It is very simple to make your rubbings into bookmarks.

Simply stick them onto strips of white or coloured card. When the glue has dried, cover them with clear, self-adhesive plastic.

You could also use leather or fabric instead of card. Fray the ends of the material or cut the leather into a fringe to make it more interesting.

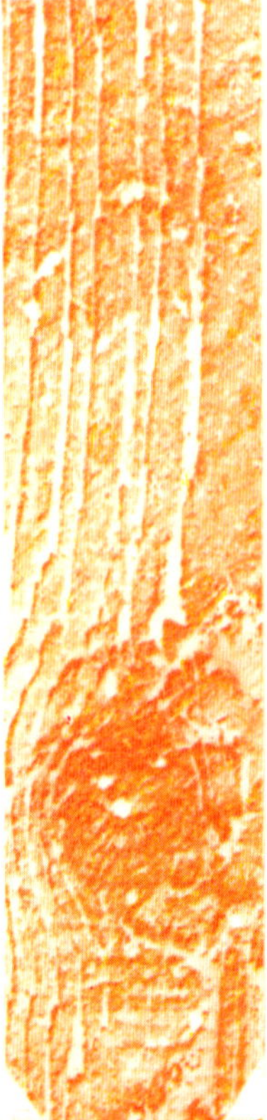

Making greetings cards

On the facing page are some ideas for decorating cards with your rubbings.

Designs can be made especially to suit your friends and relations by choosing objects to rub that you know they would like. Or, you could draw designs on card and cut them out, or you could use animals, flowers, ships, names and numbers printed on chocolate boxes, old cards and similar things. Paste them onto a piece of card and leave them to dry. Cover them with lining or architects' detail paper, and rub in the usual way with one or more coloured crayons. Mount the rubbing on thick paper, white or coloured card. If you have rubbed over the edge of the design by mistake, cut it out before you mount it.

Excellent rubbings may be reproduced from a lino-cut.

Since this method enables you to make several rubbings from the same design, you could make many of your cards from the same original. So make sure you are perfectly satisfied with the design before you start to rub.

Index